This Book Belong To

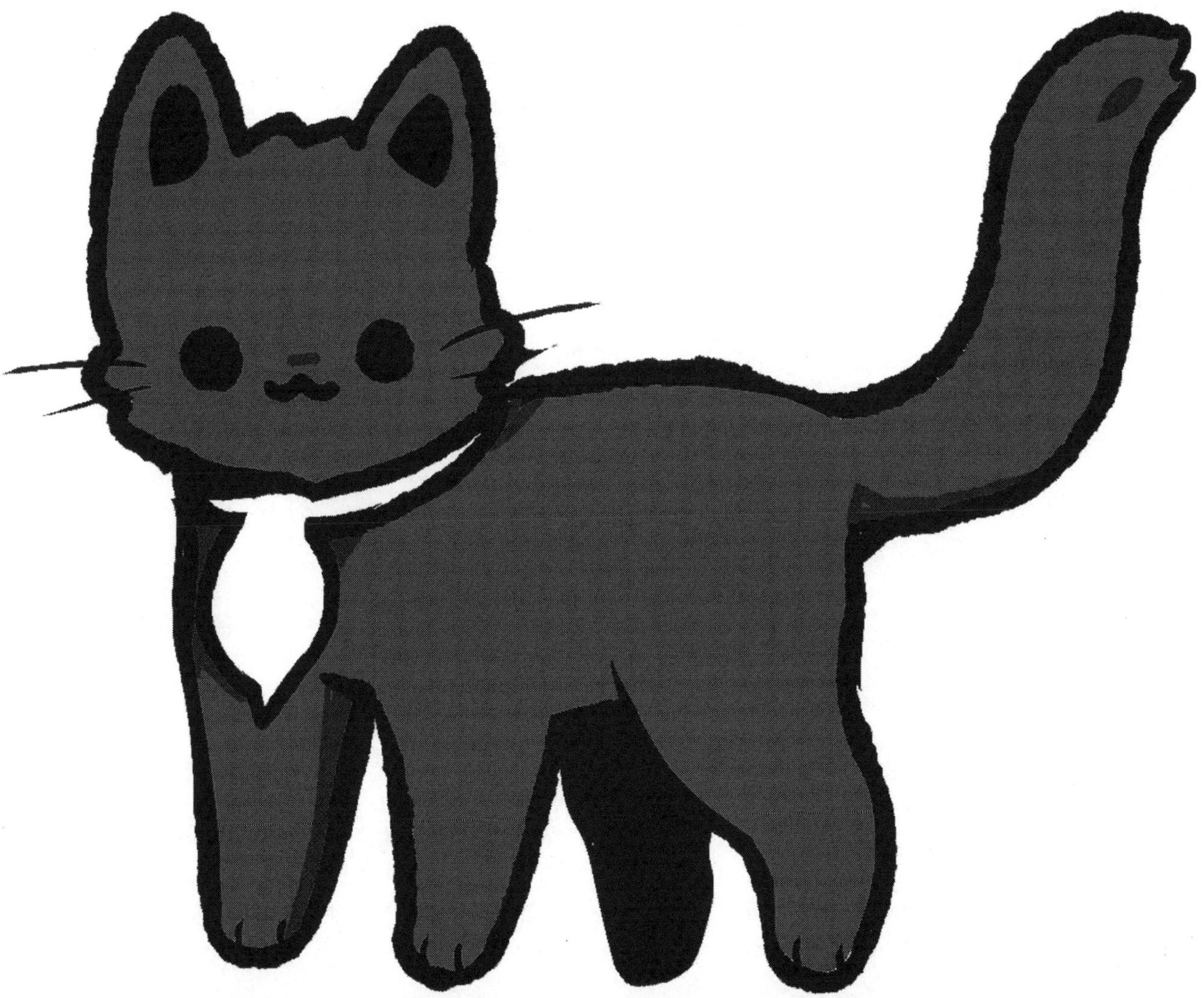

Relax and enjoy super cute cats

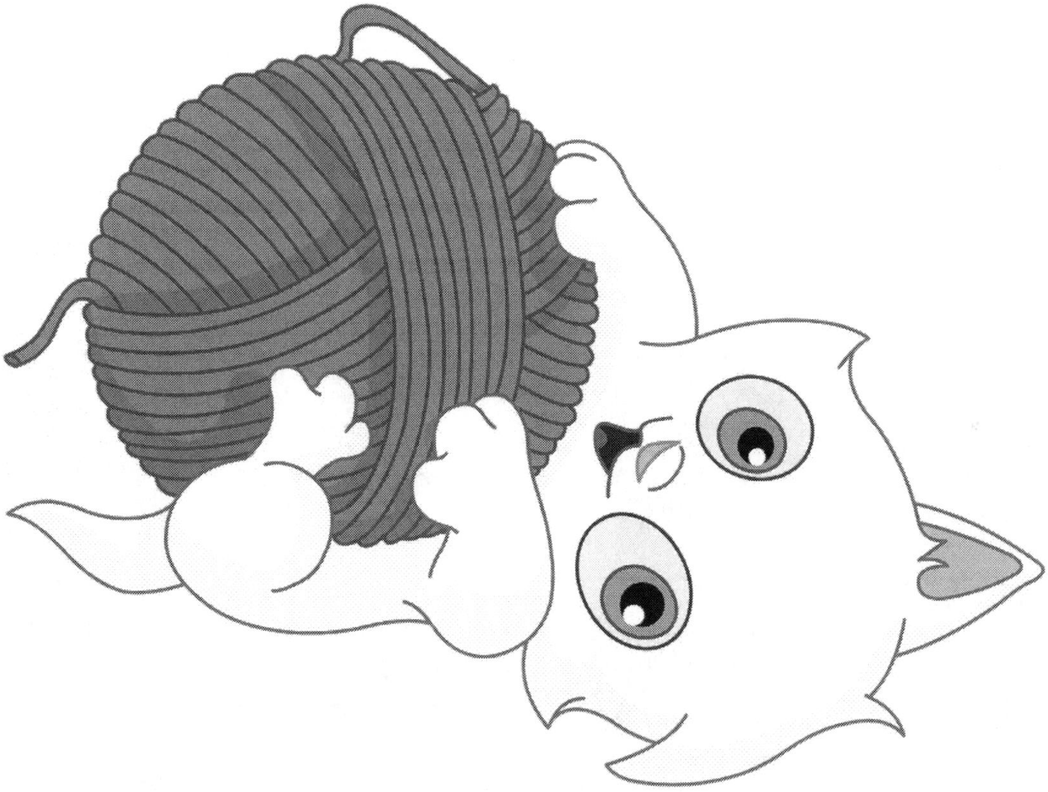

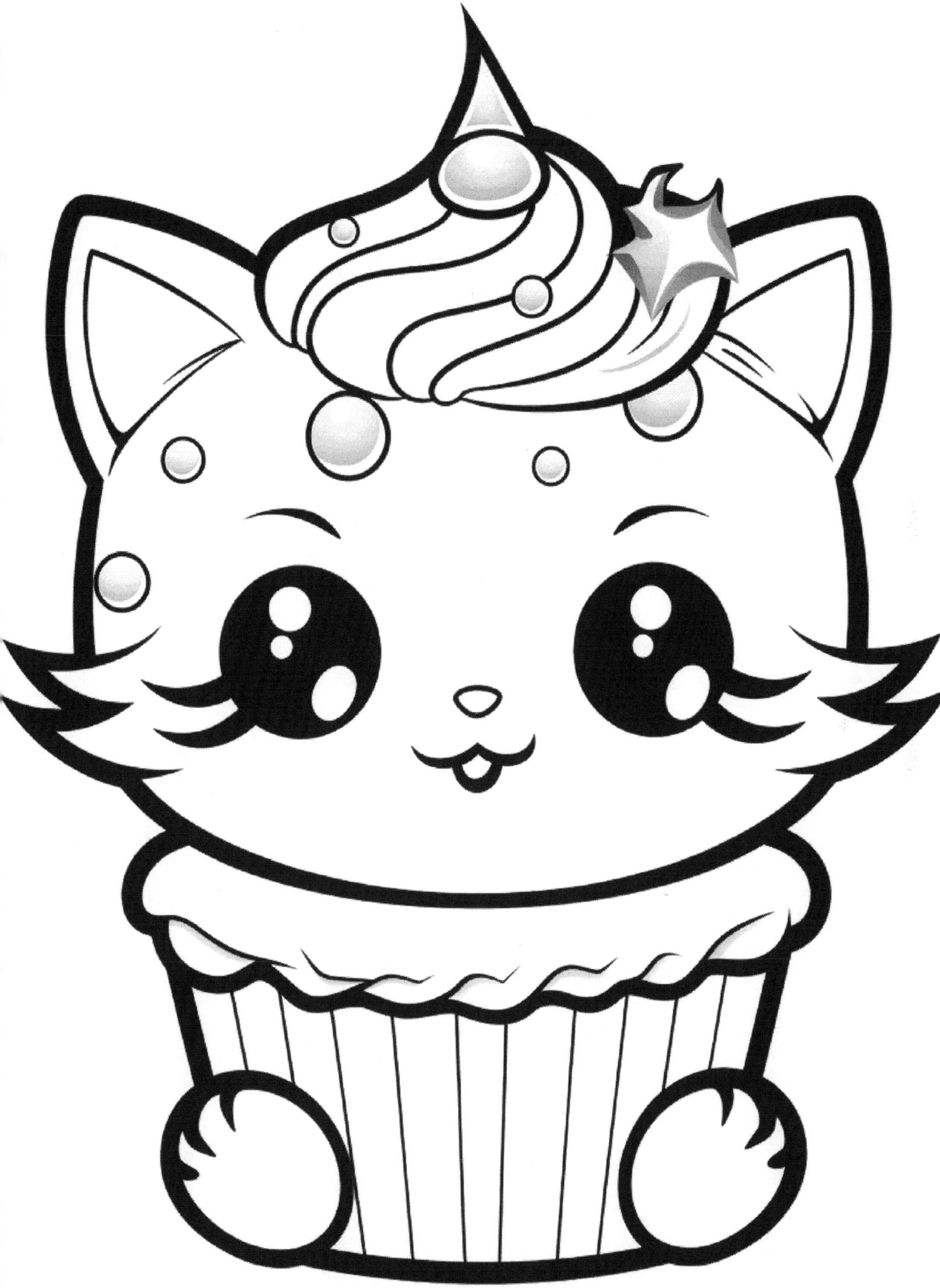

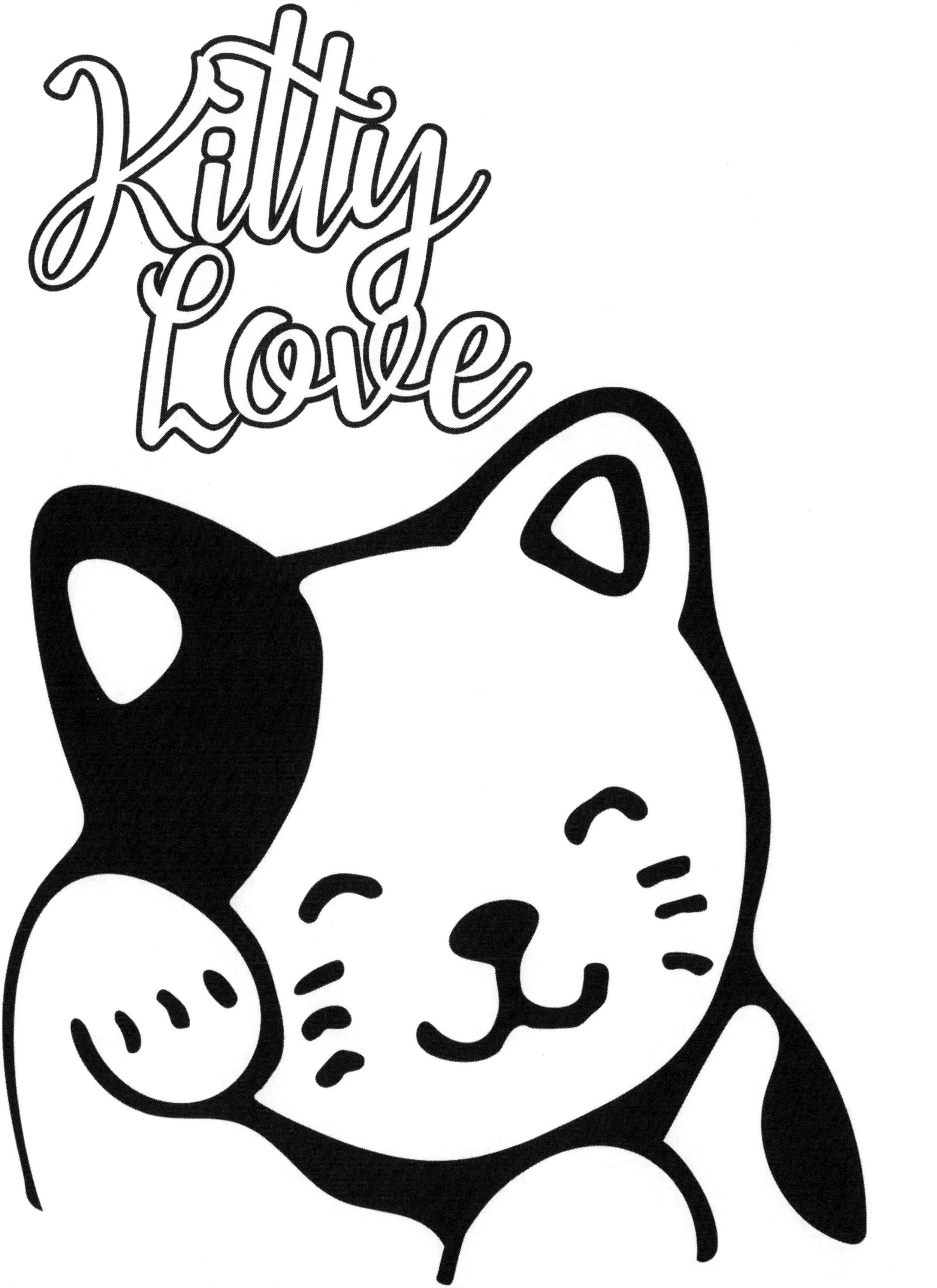
Kitty Love

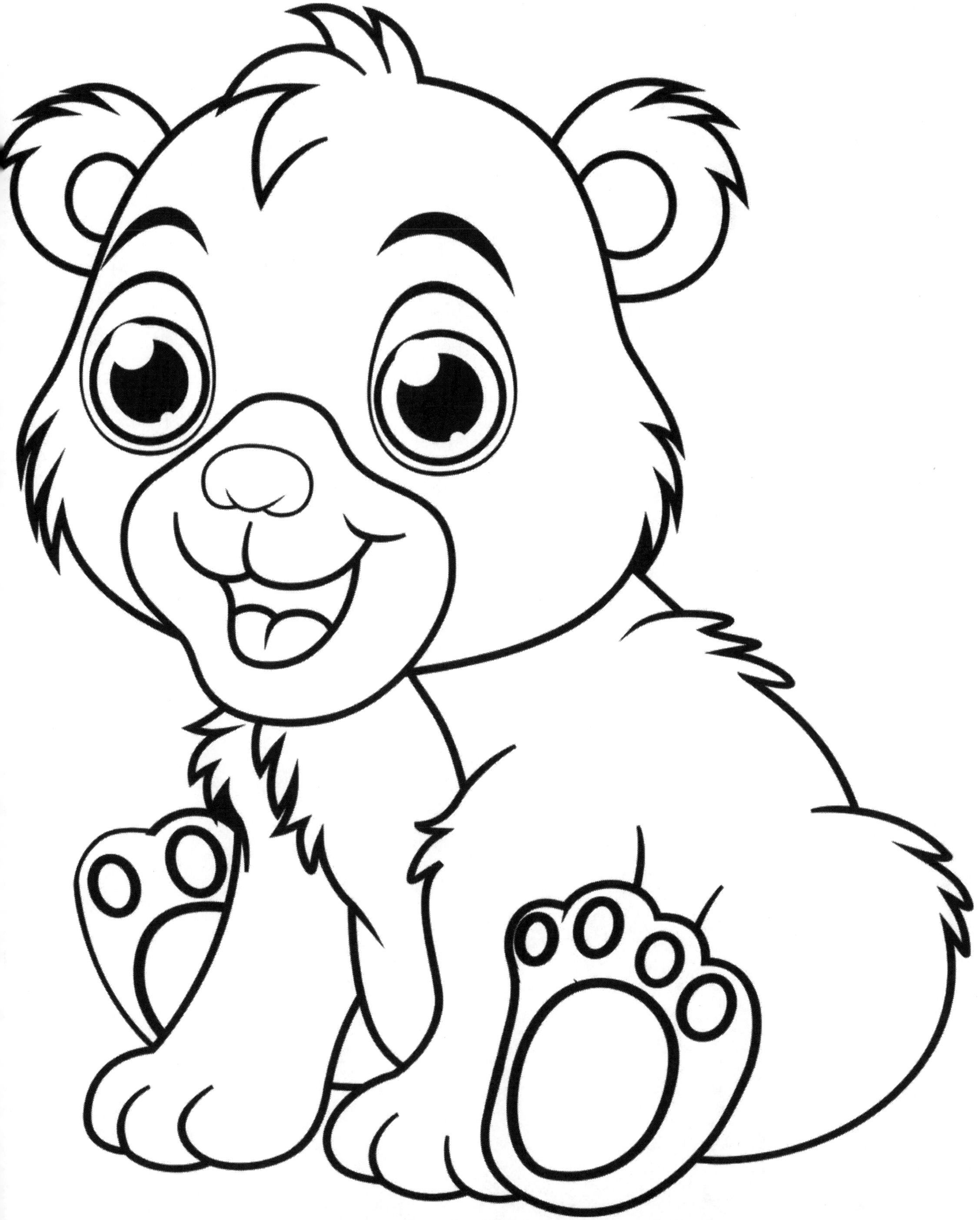

So cute

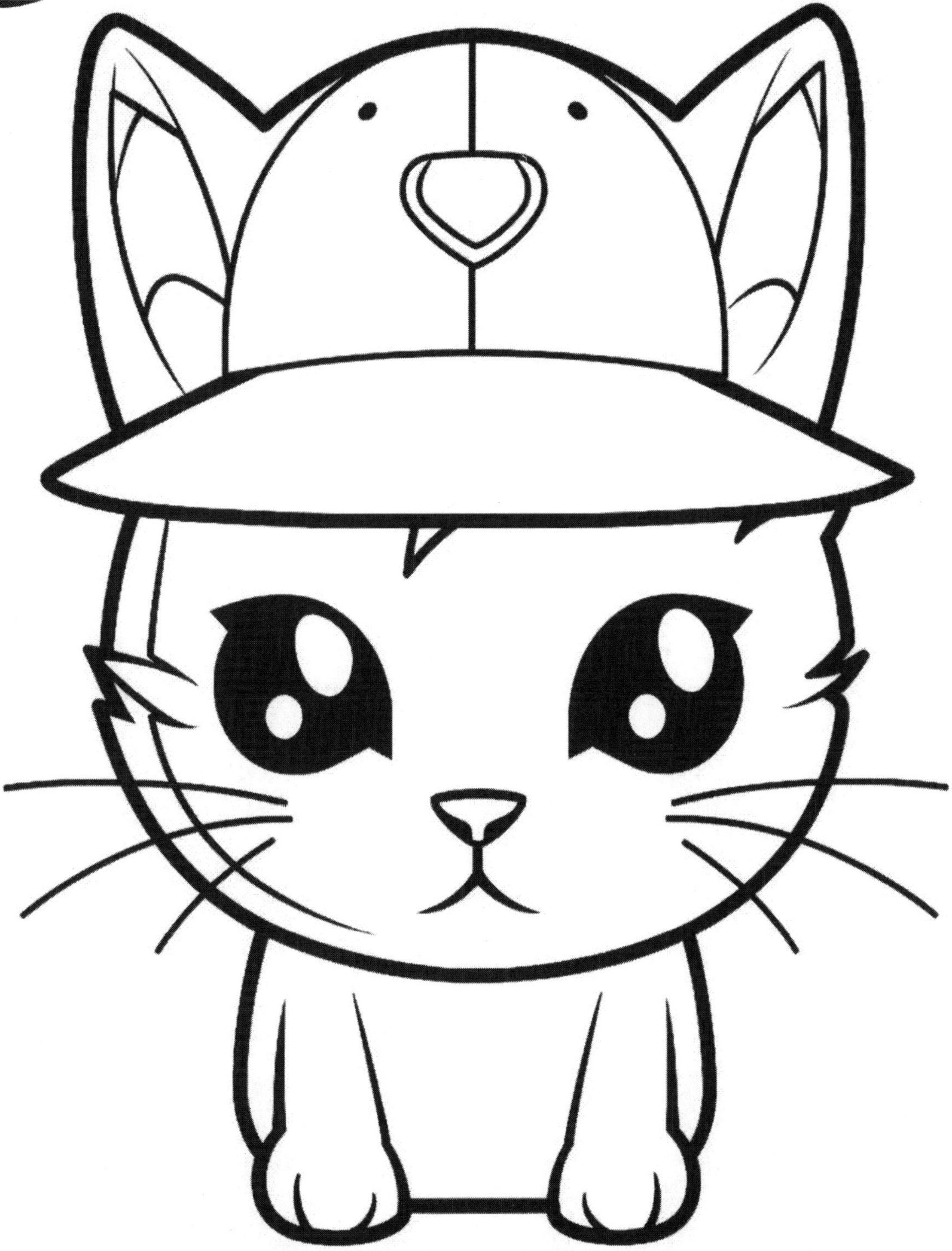

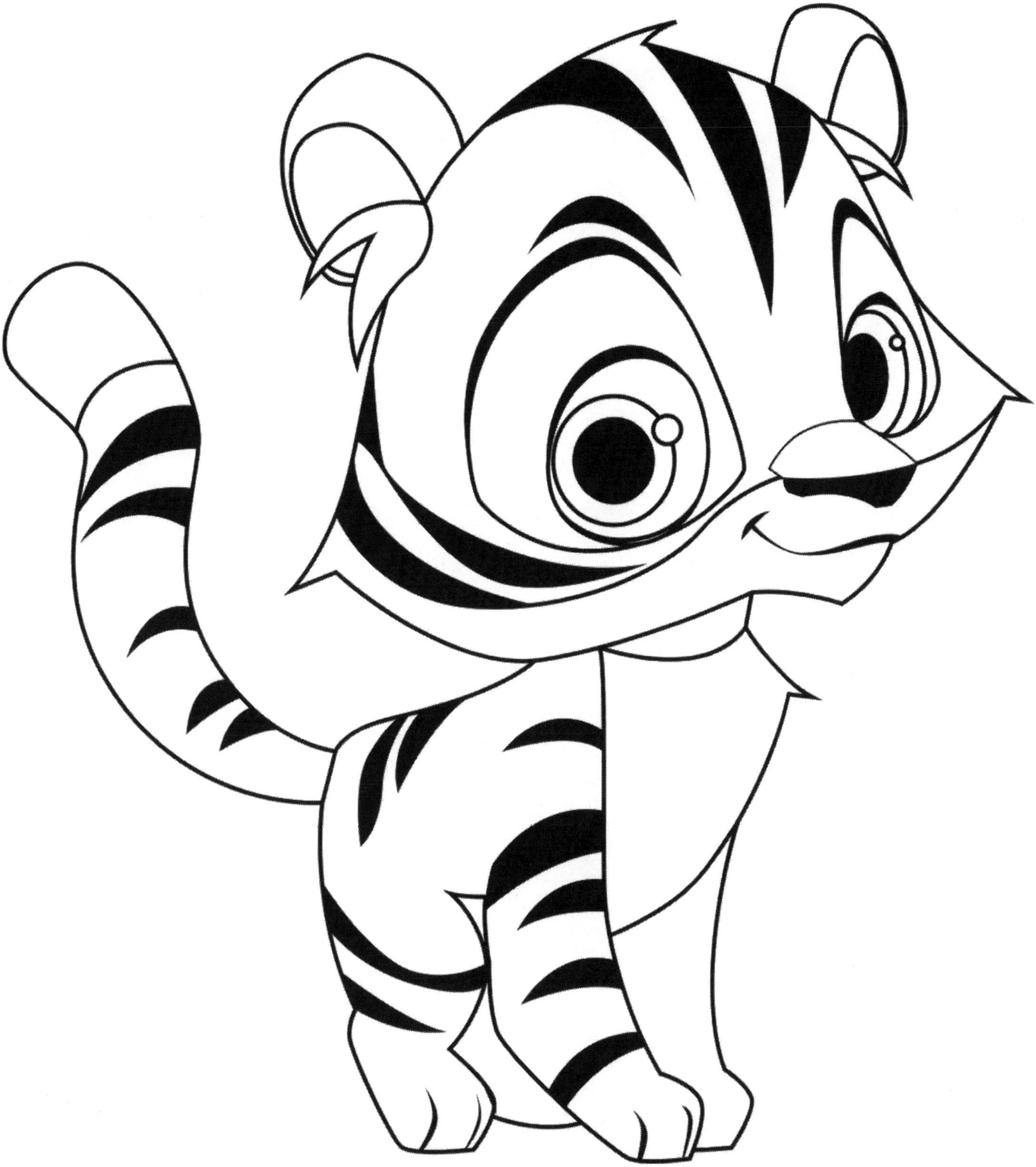

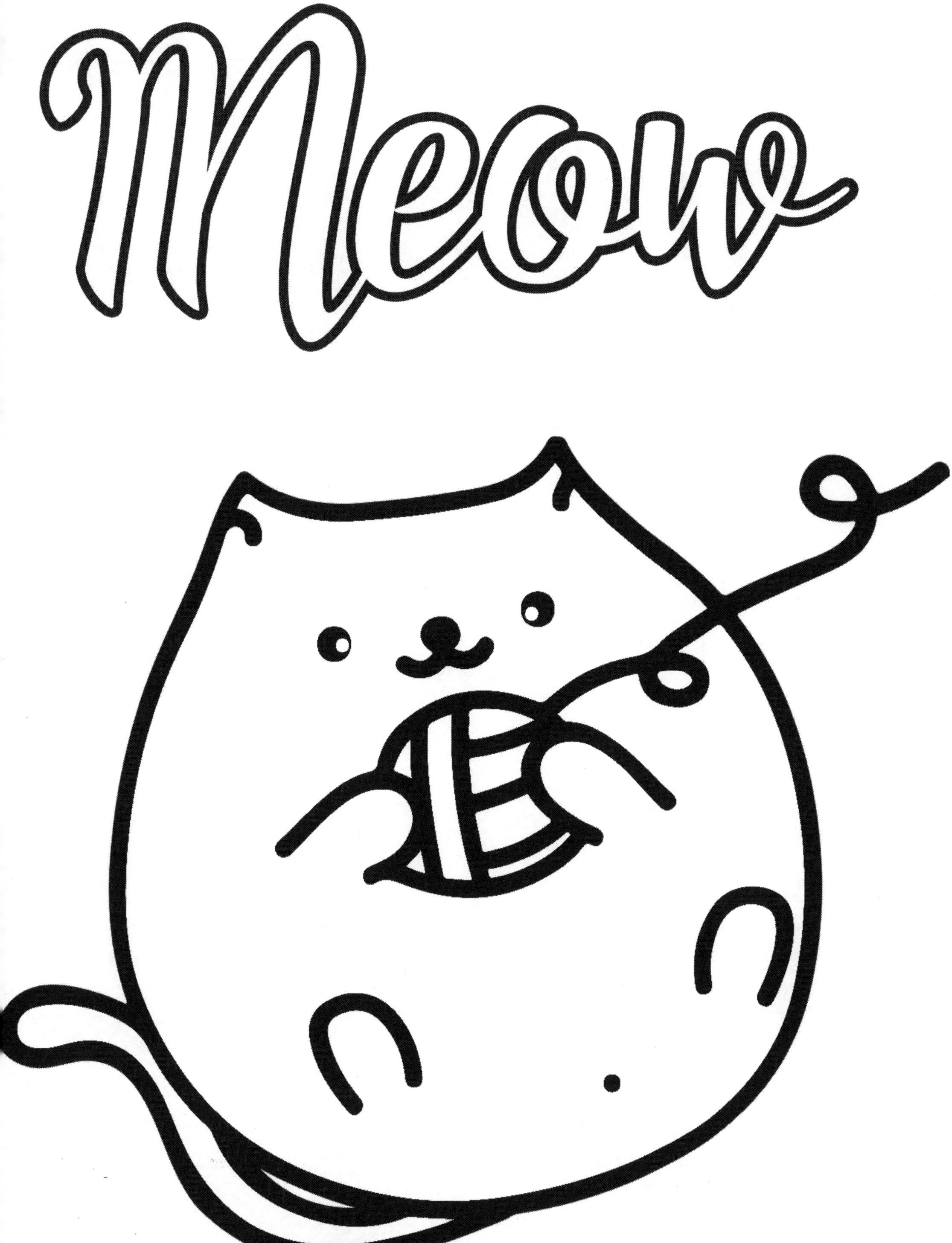
Meow

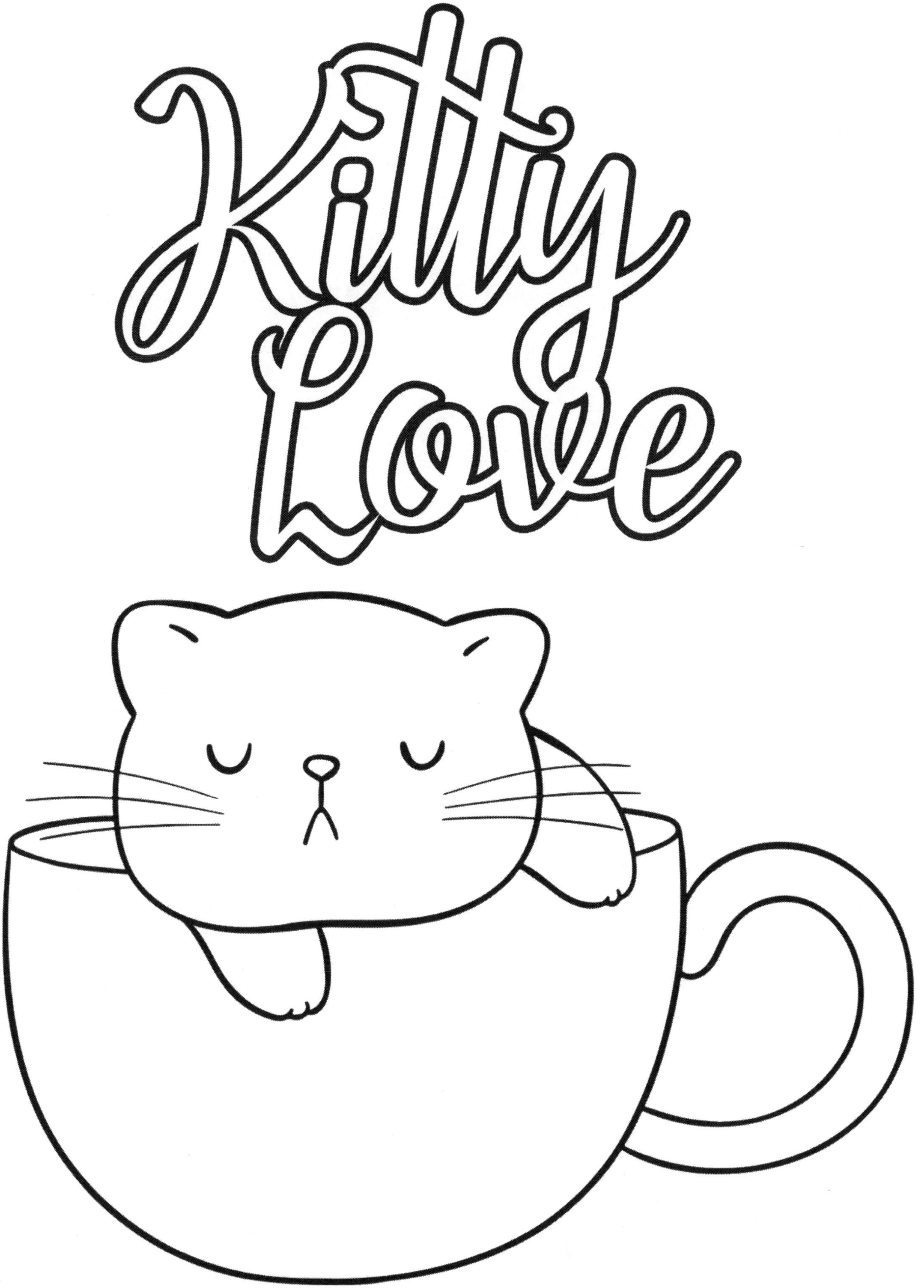
Kitty Love

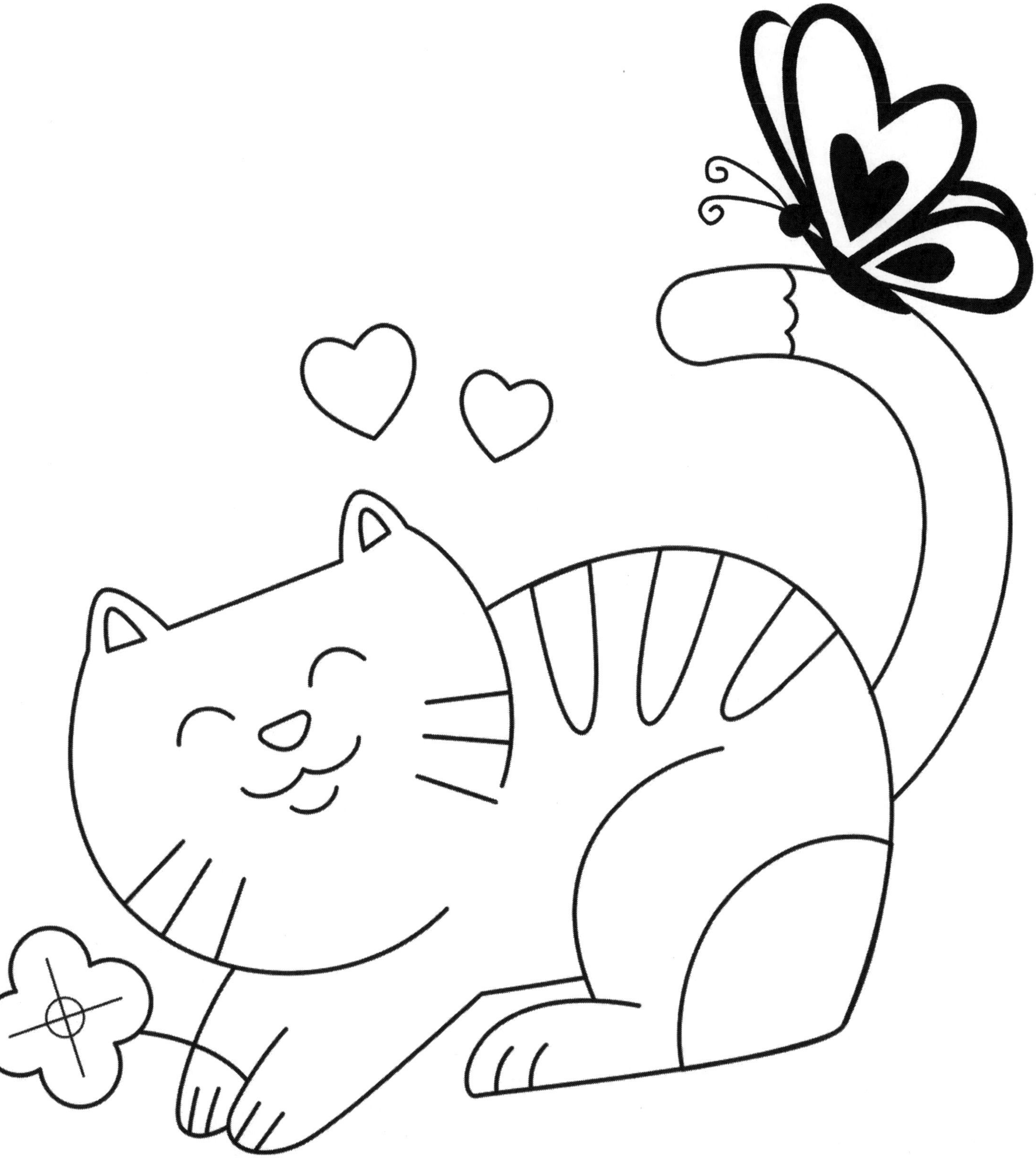

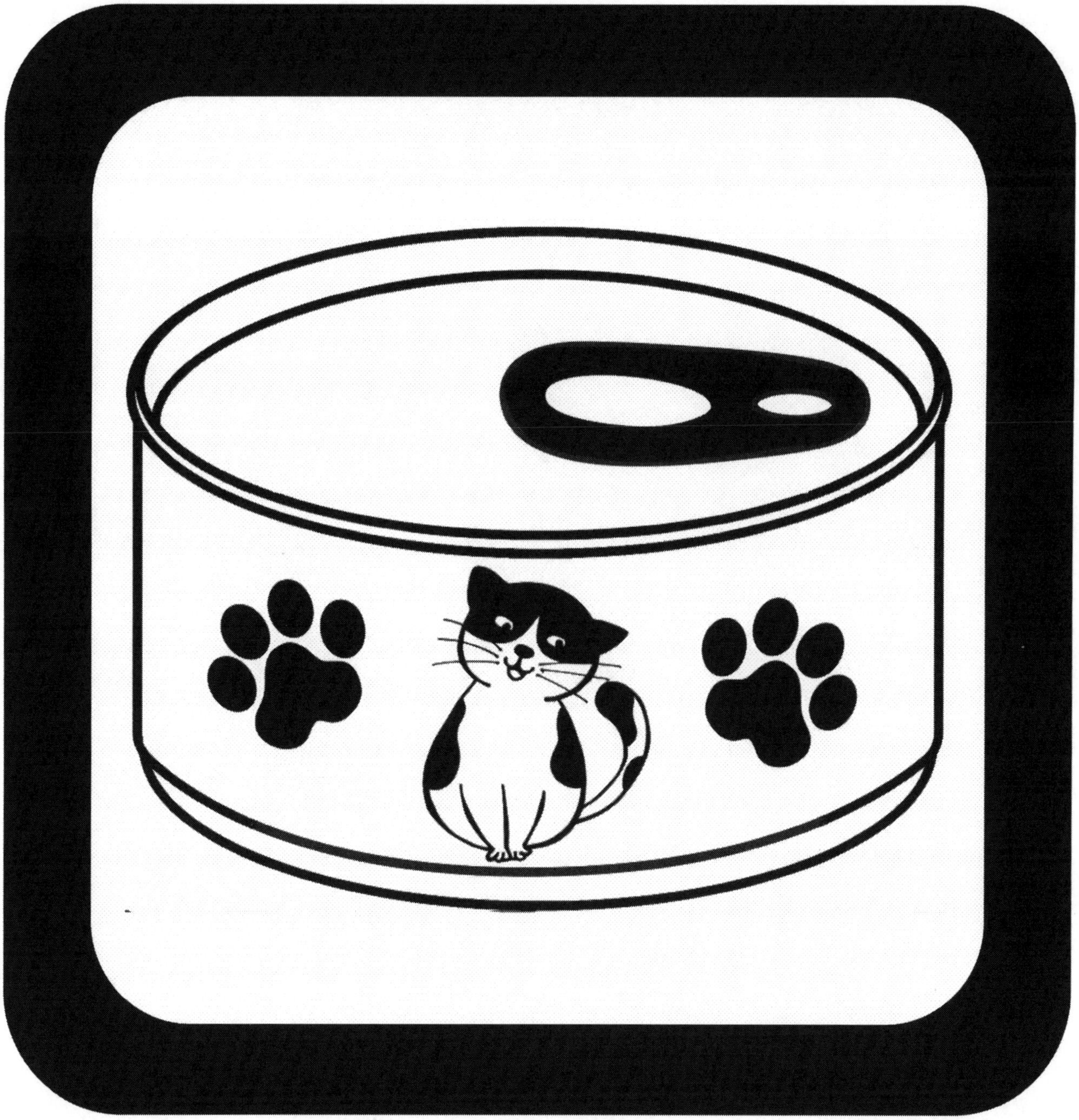

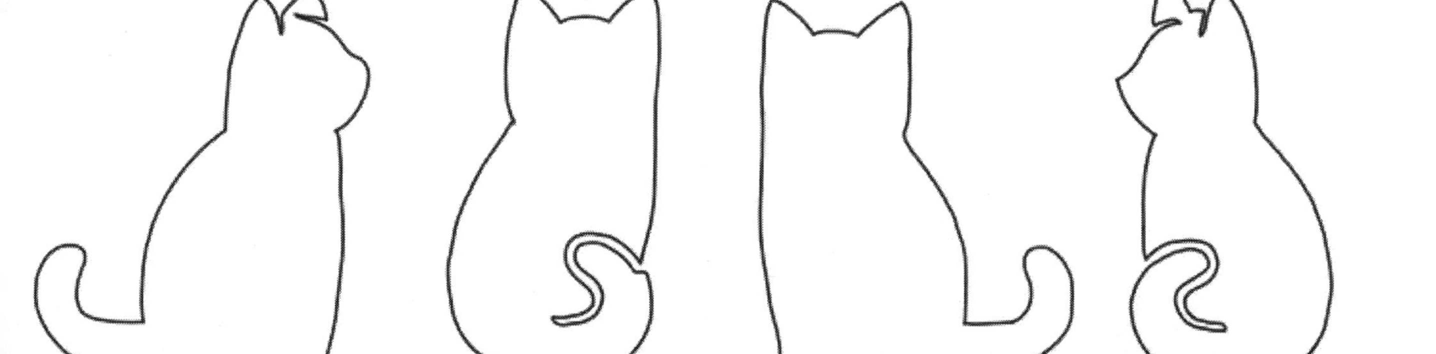

Fancy

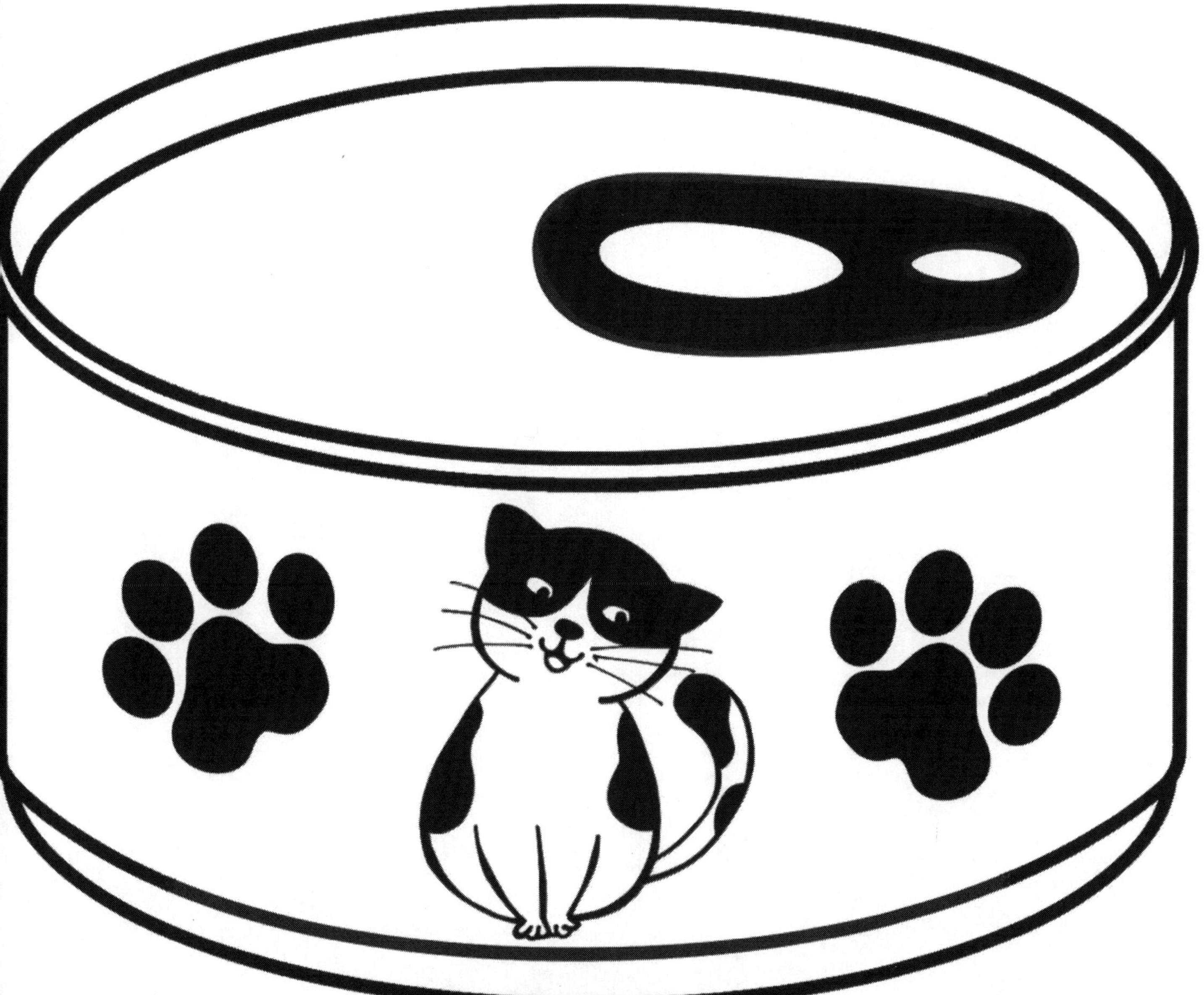

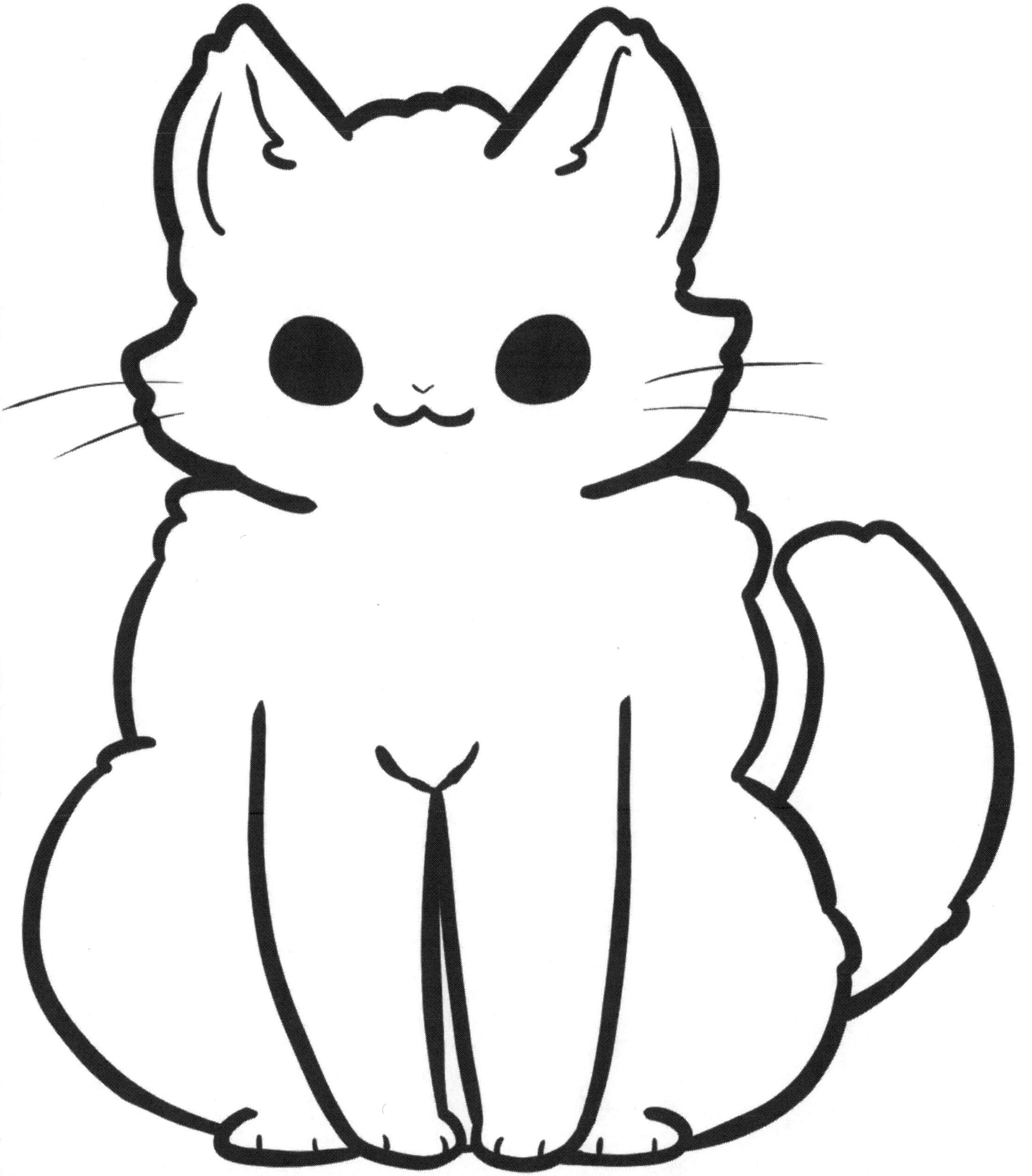

So cute

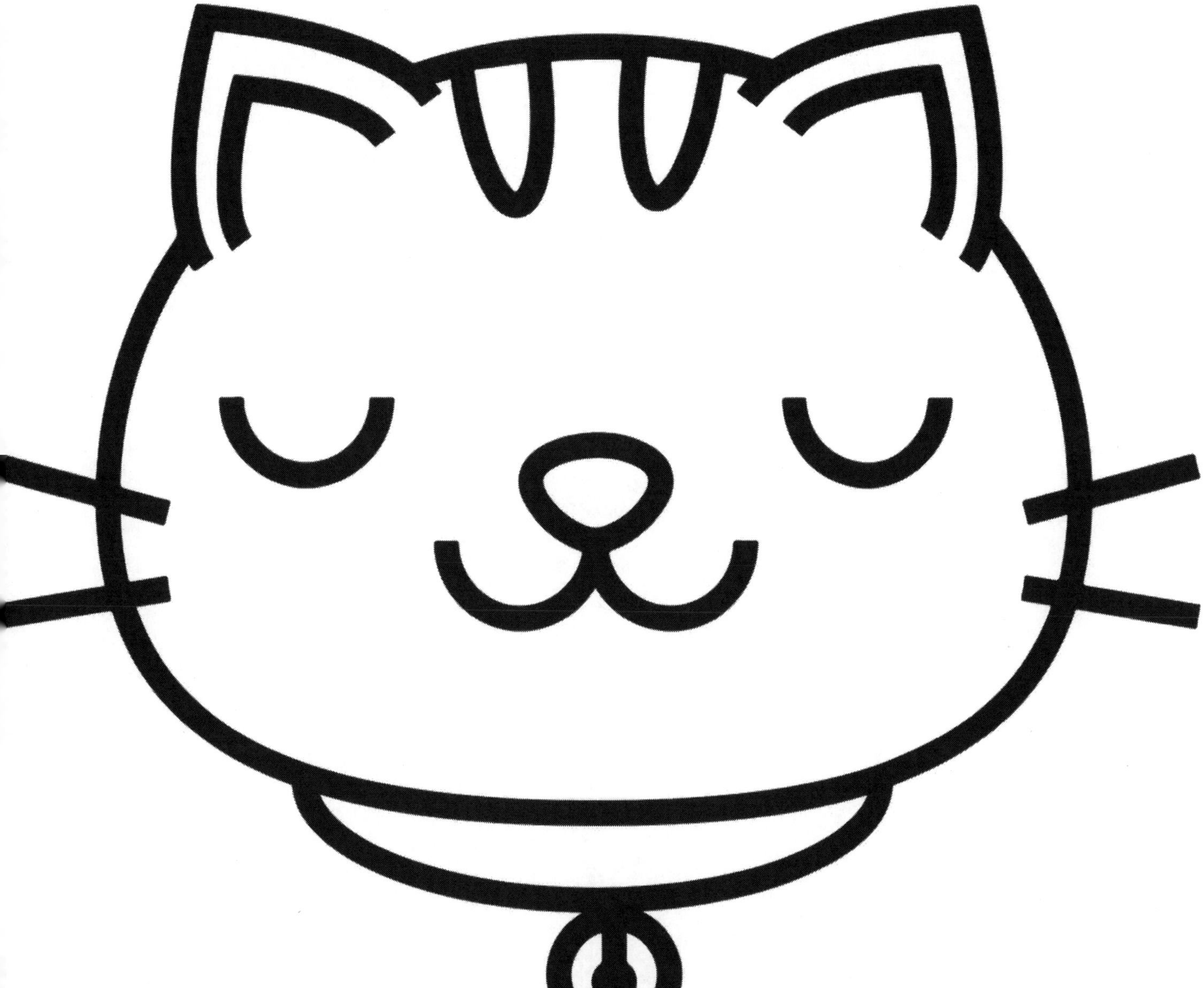

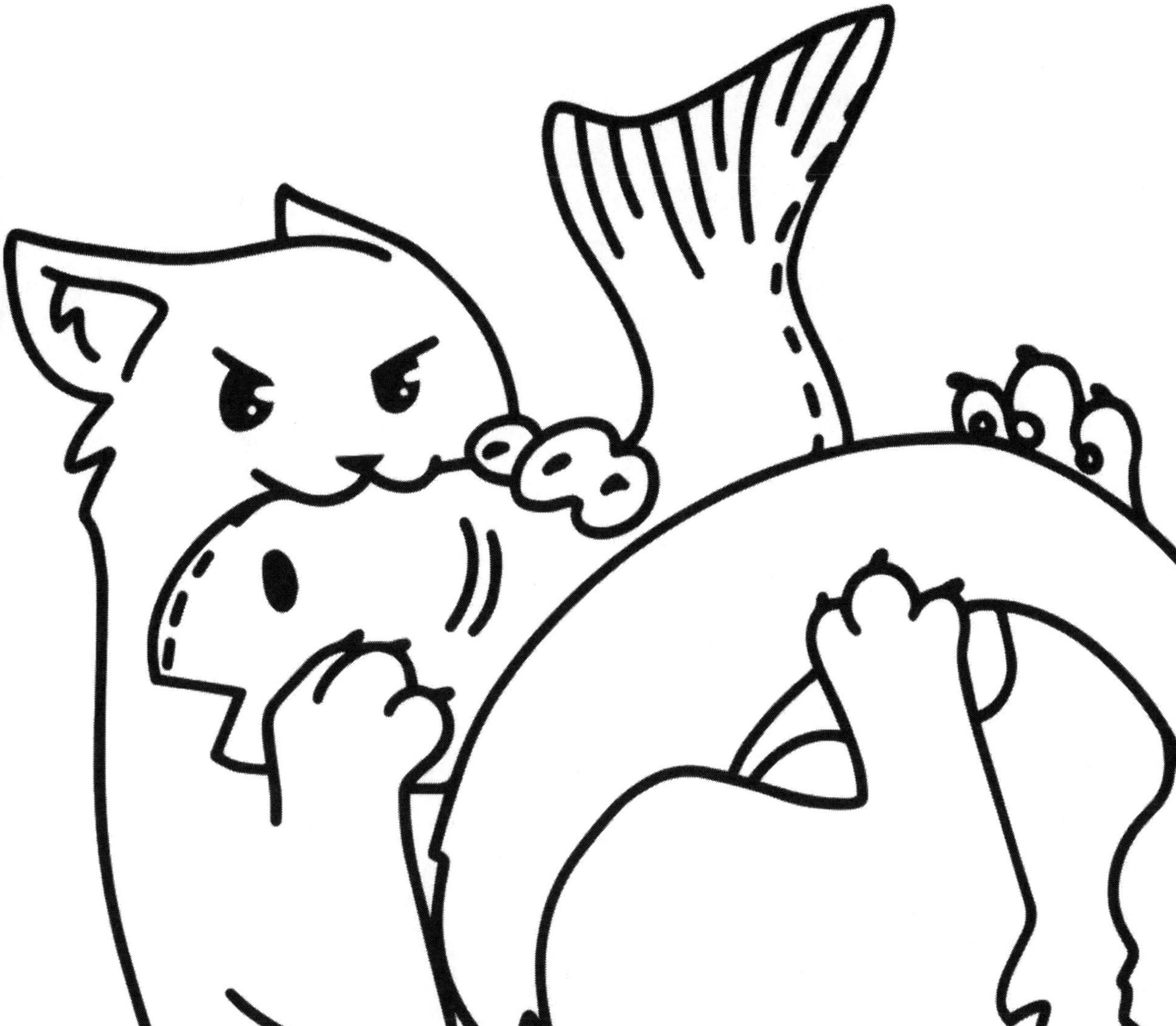

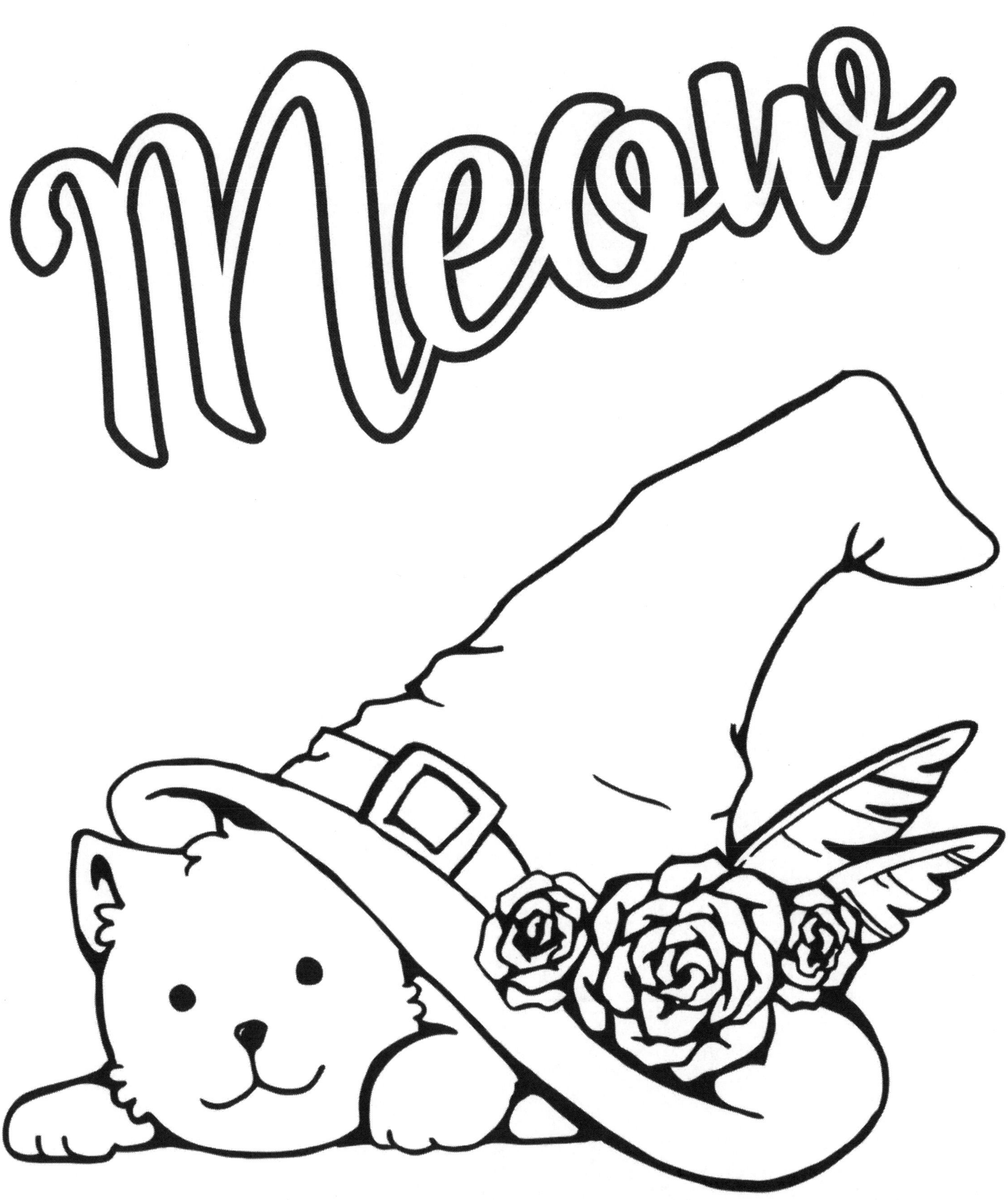
Meow

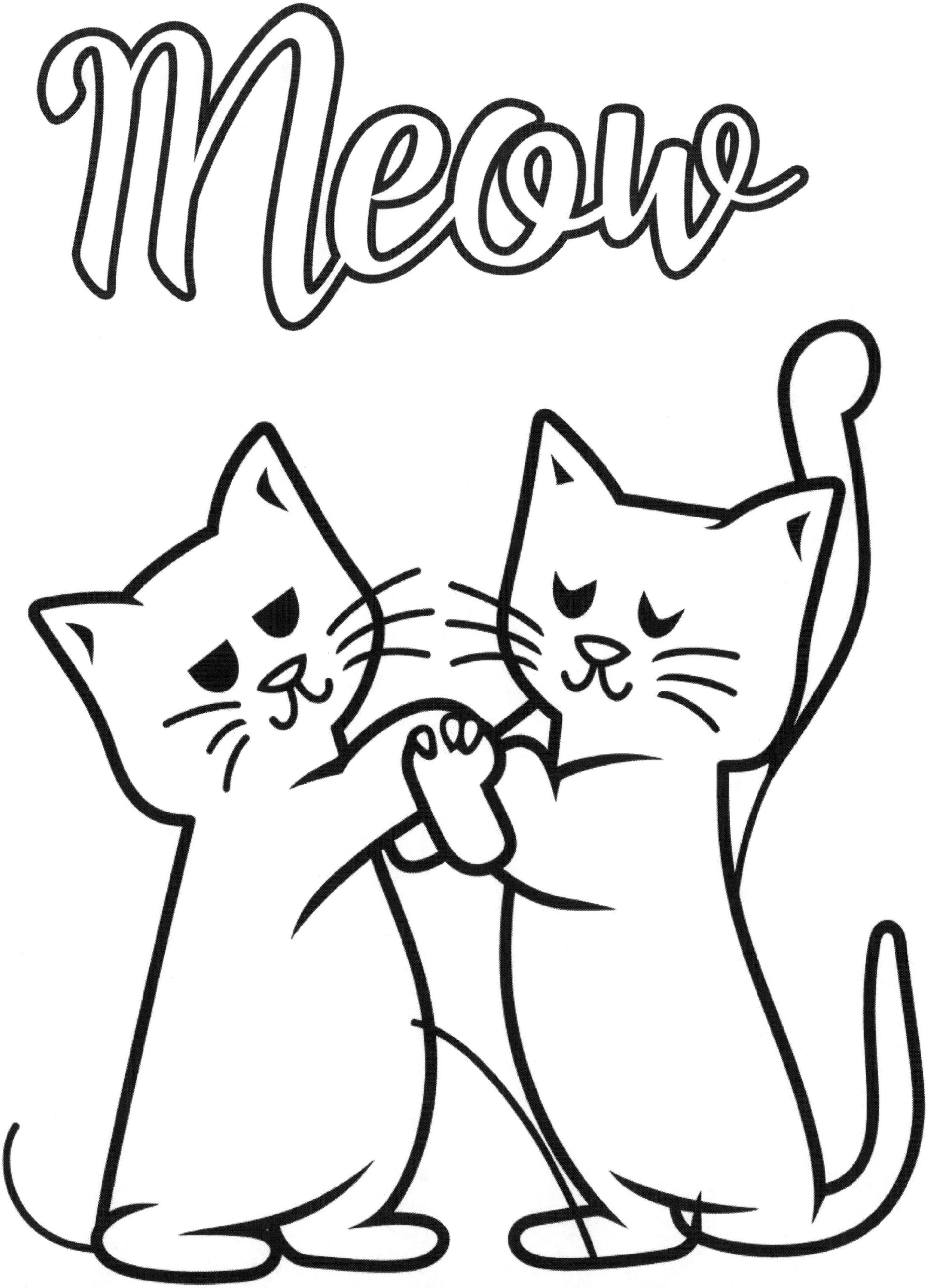
Meow

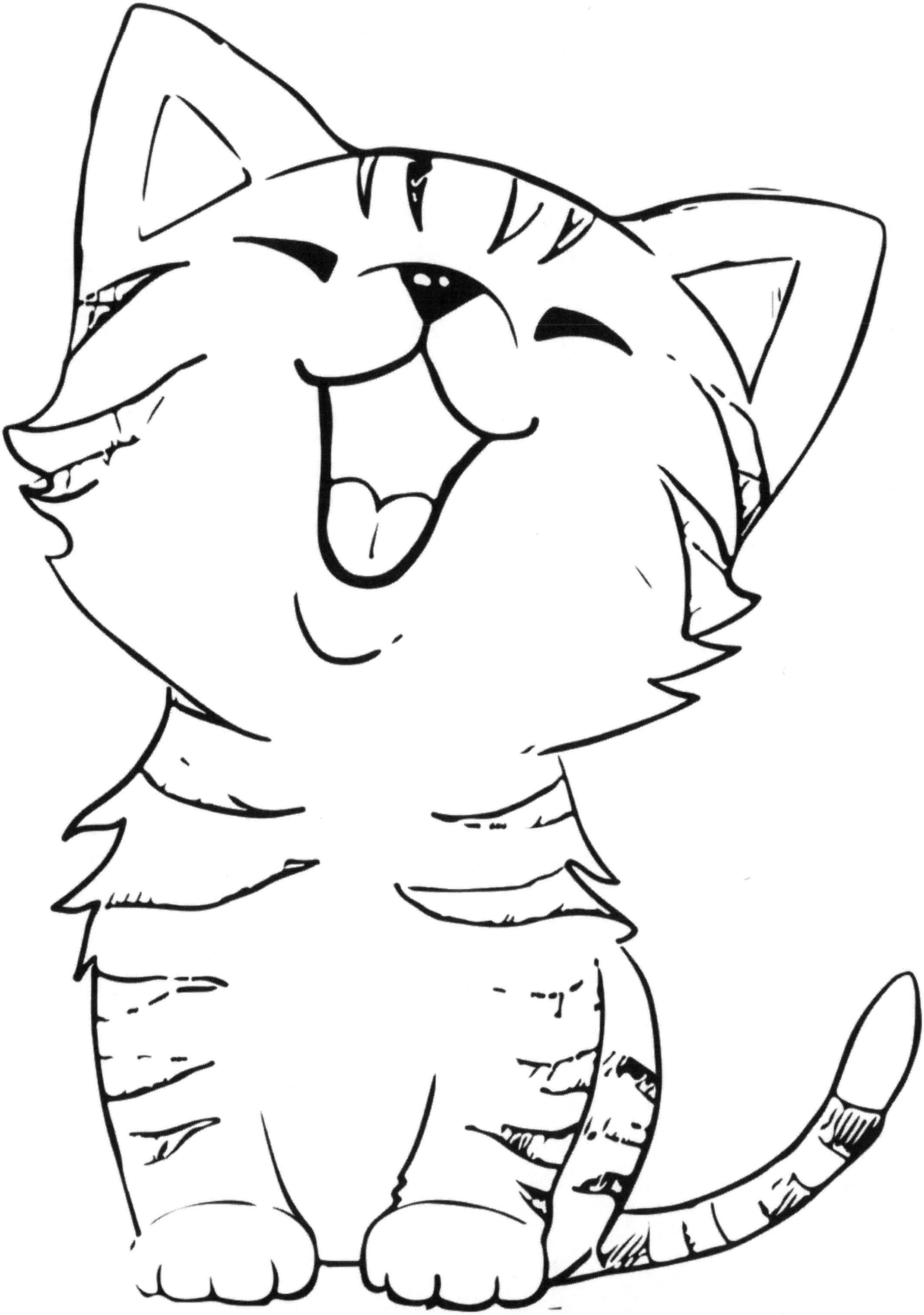

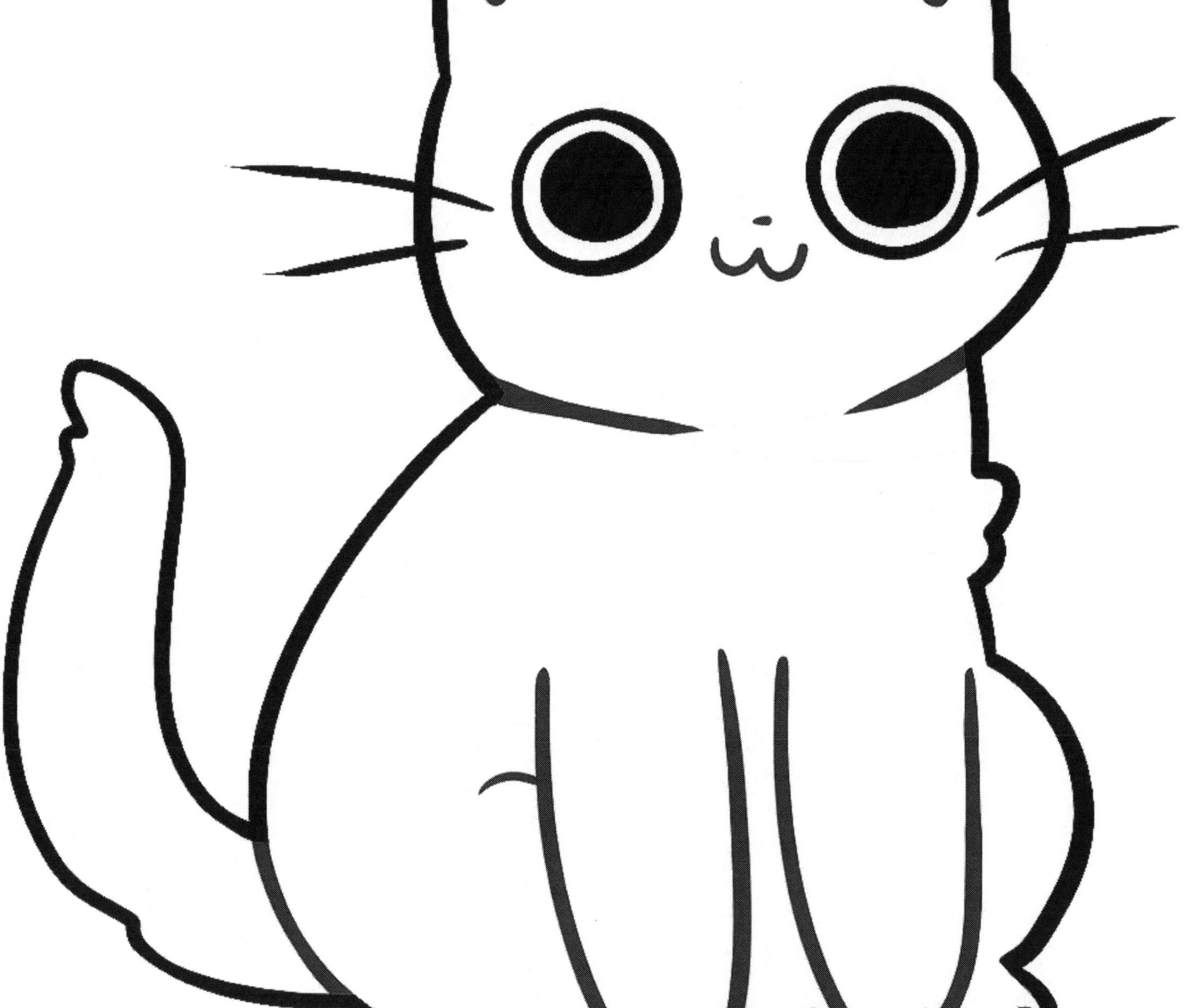

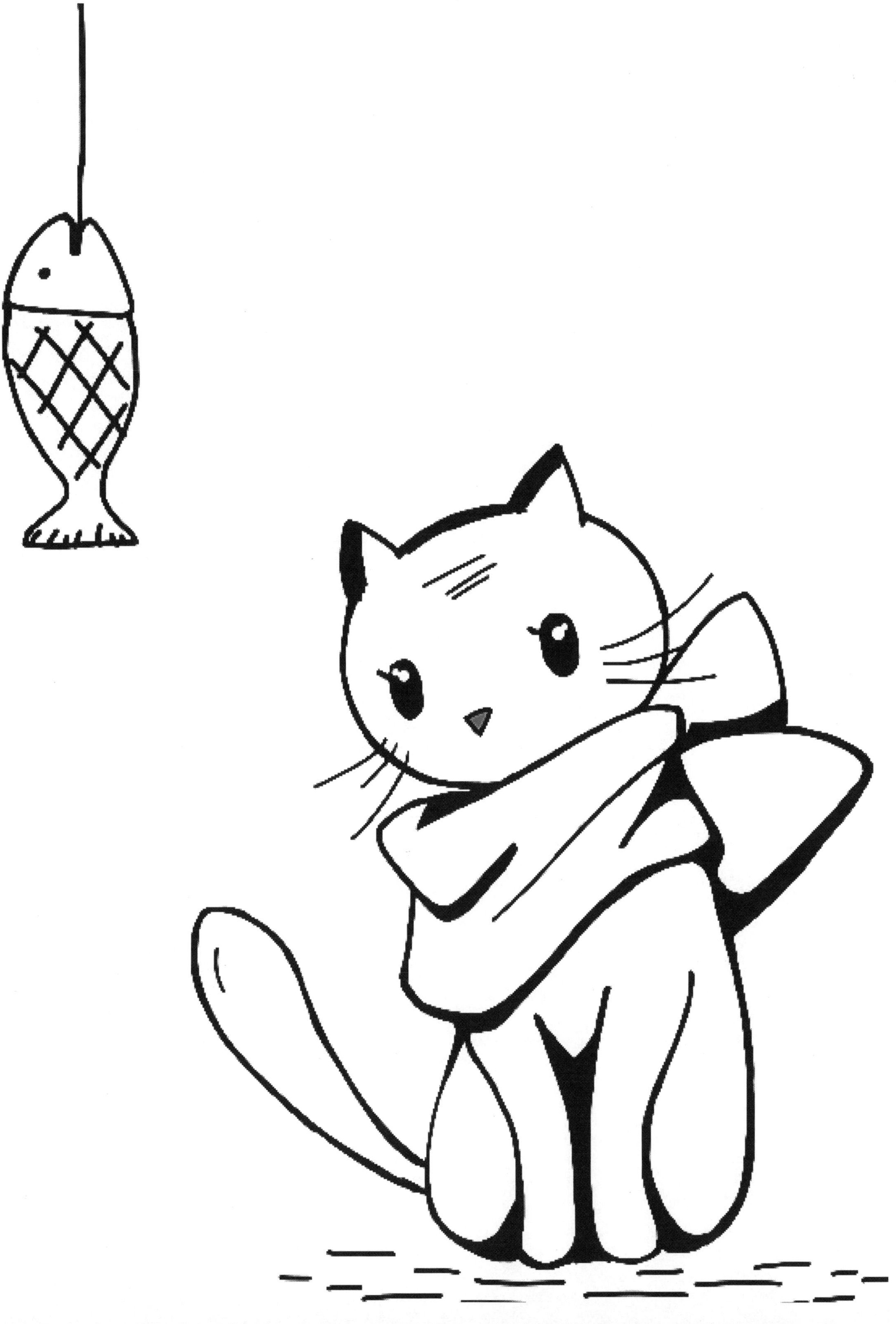

Meow

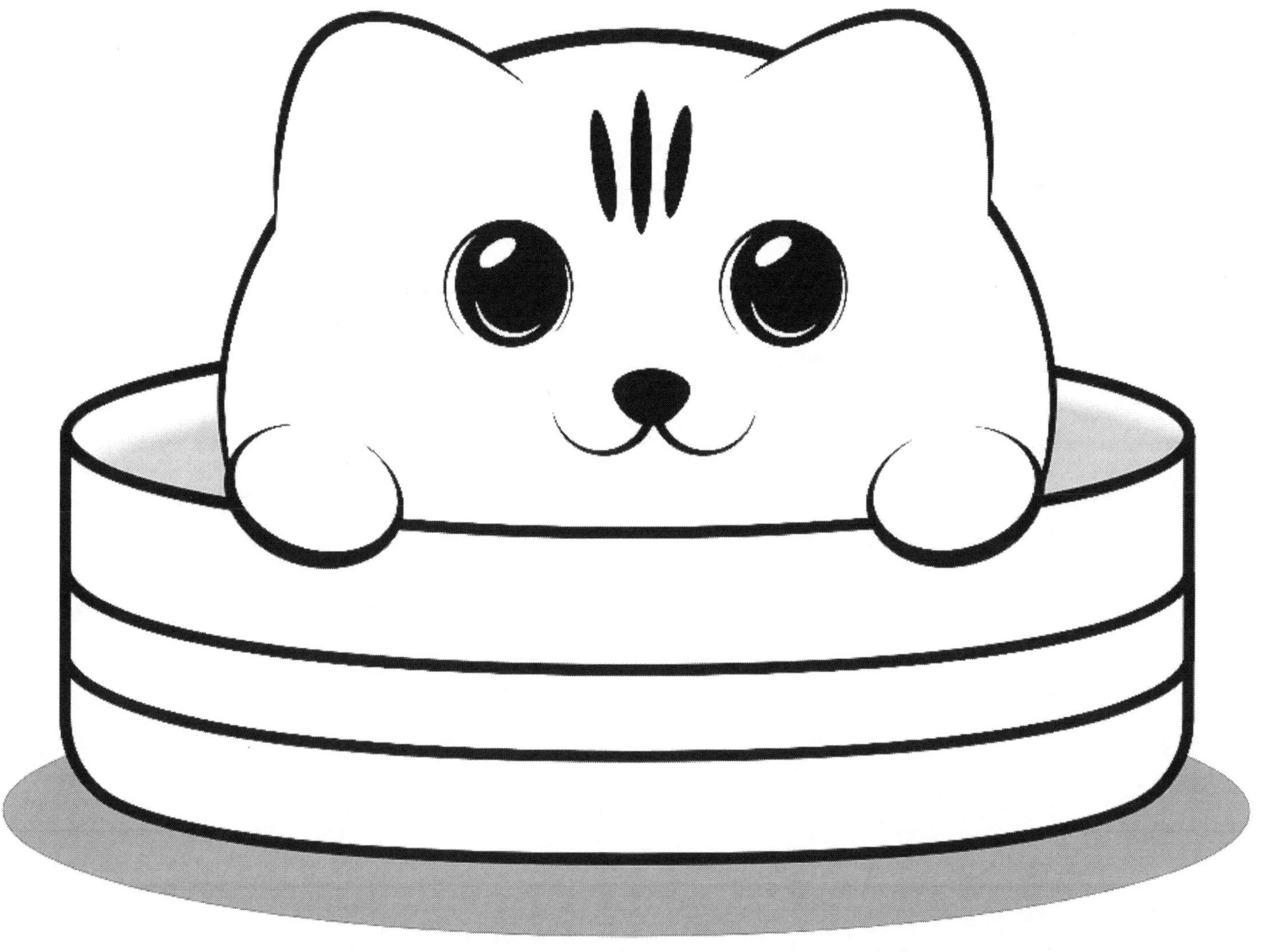

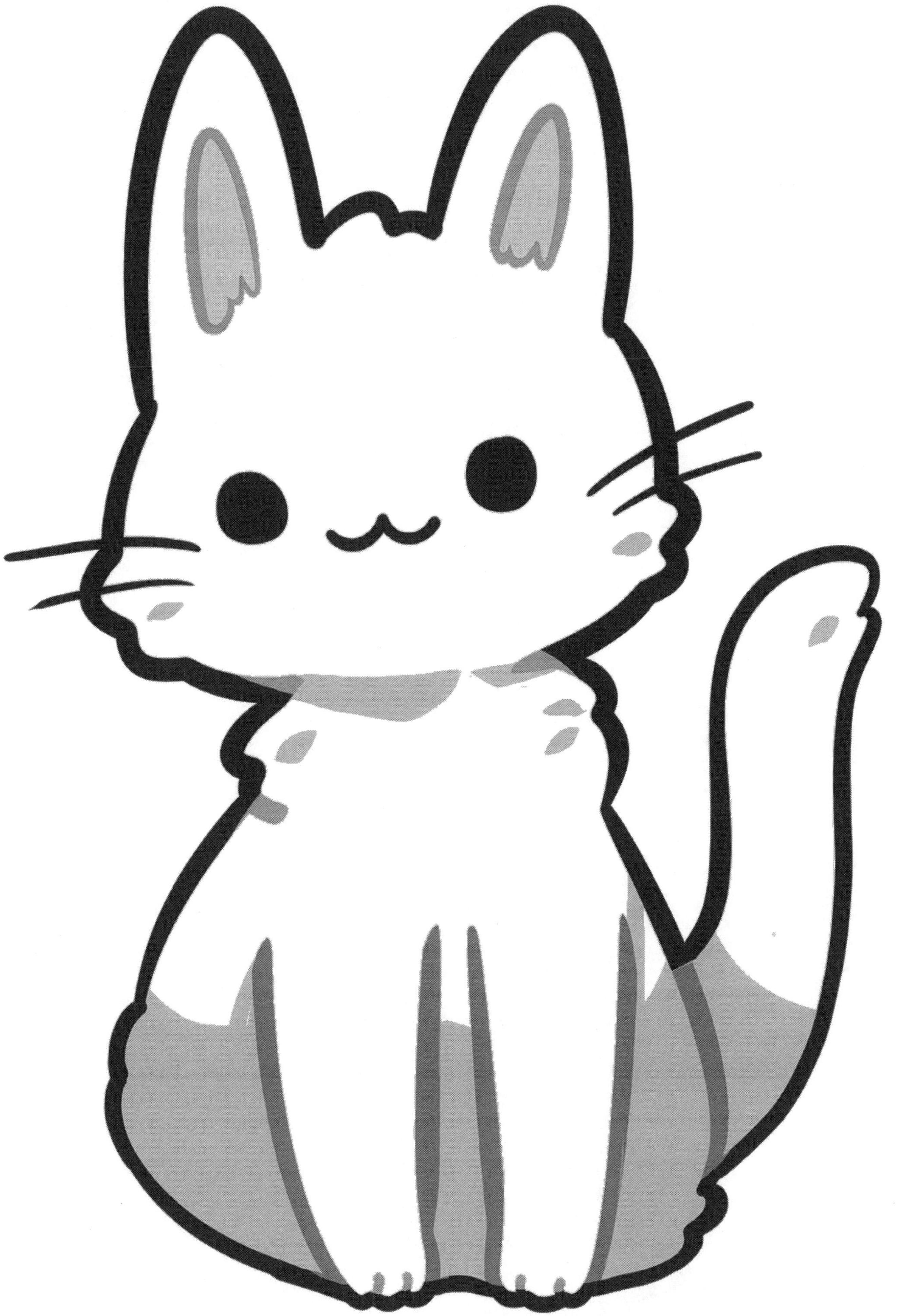

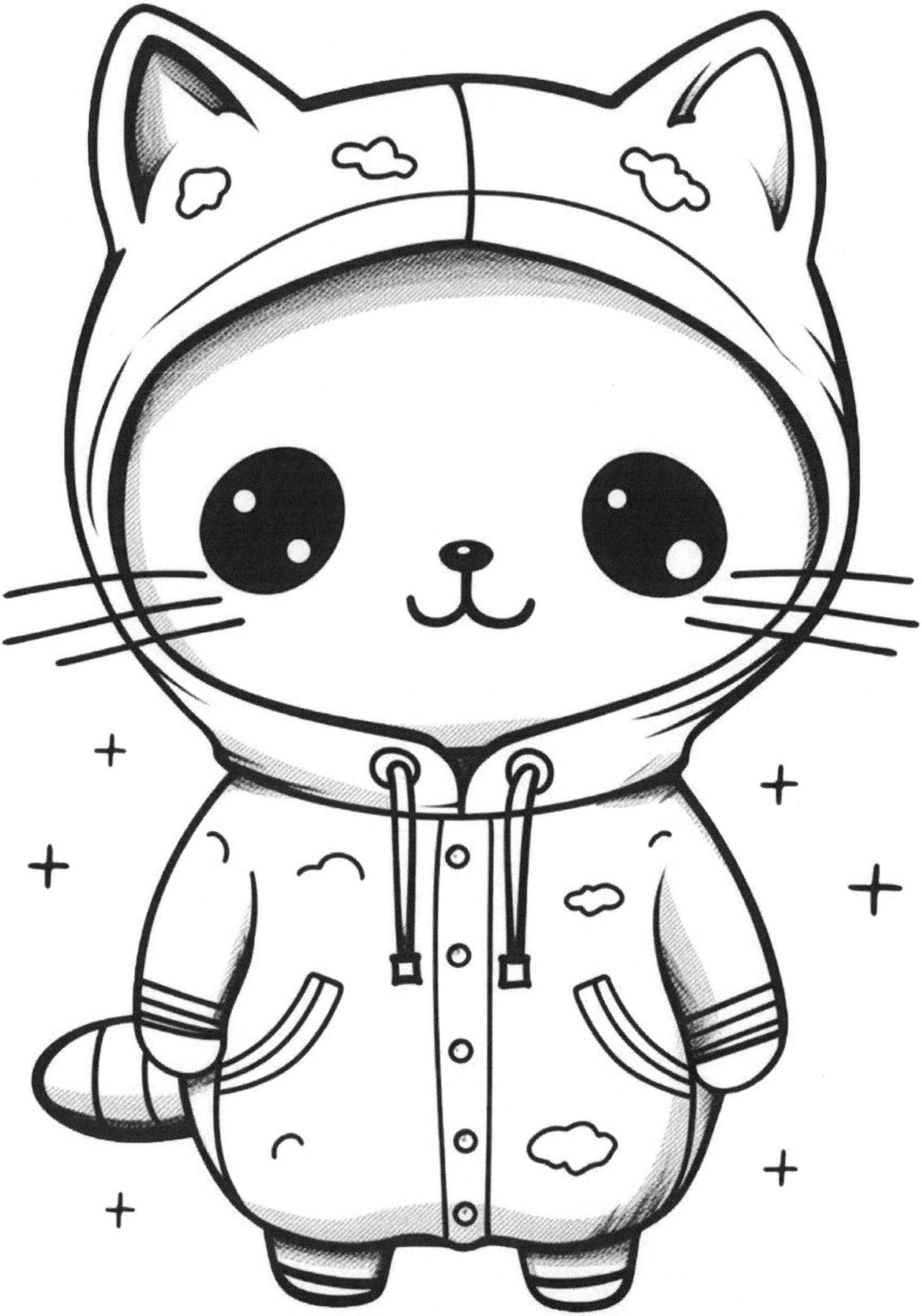

Yarn

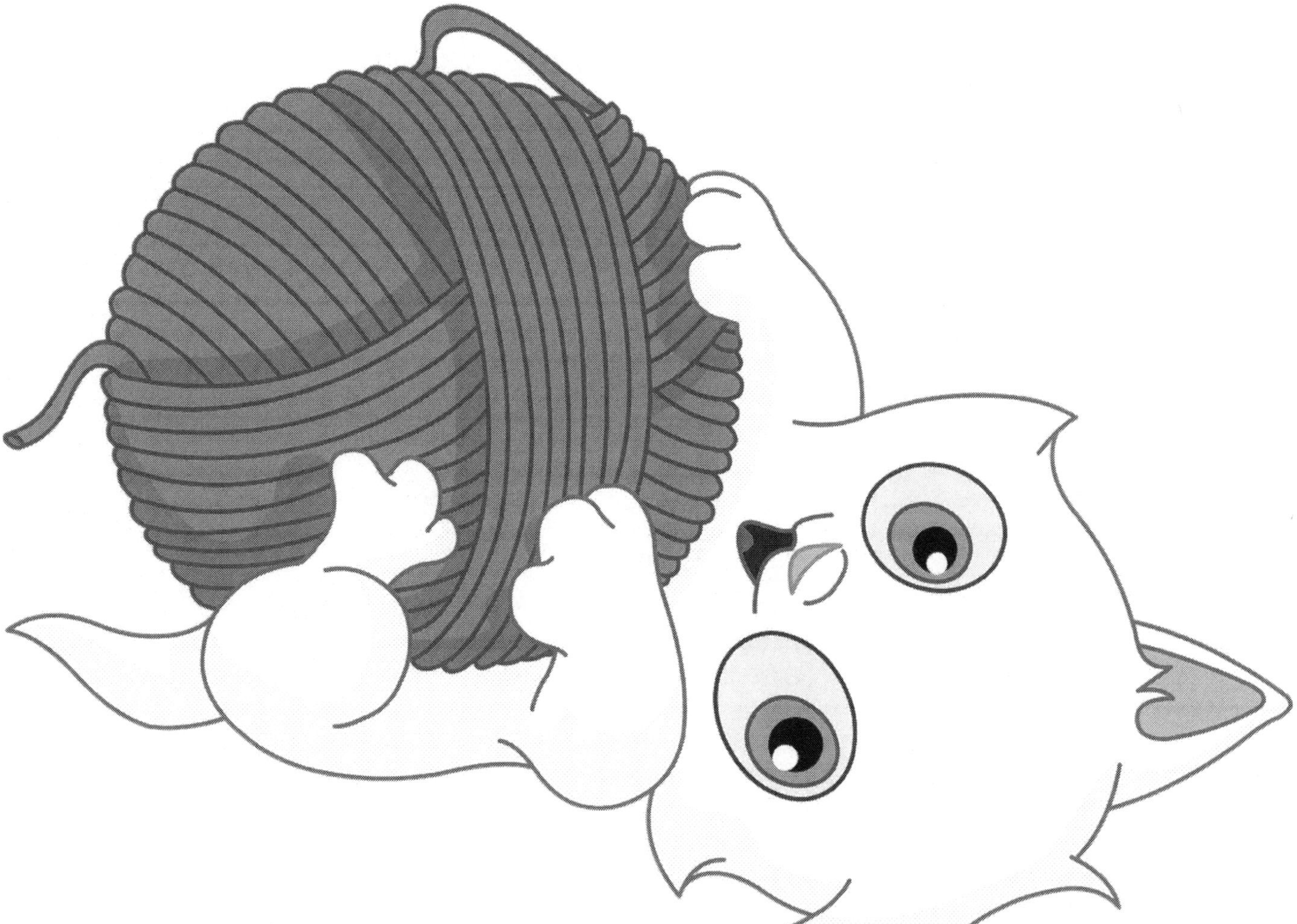

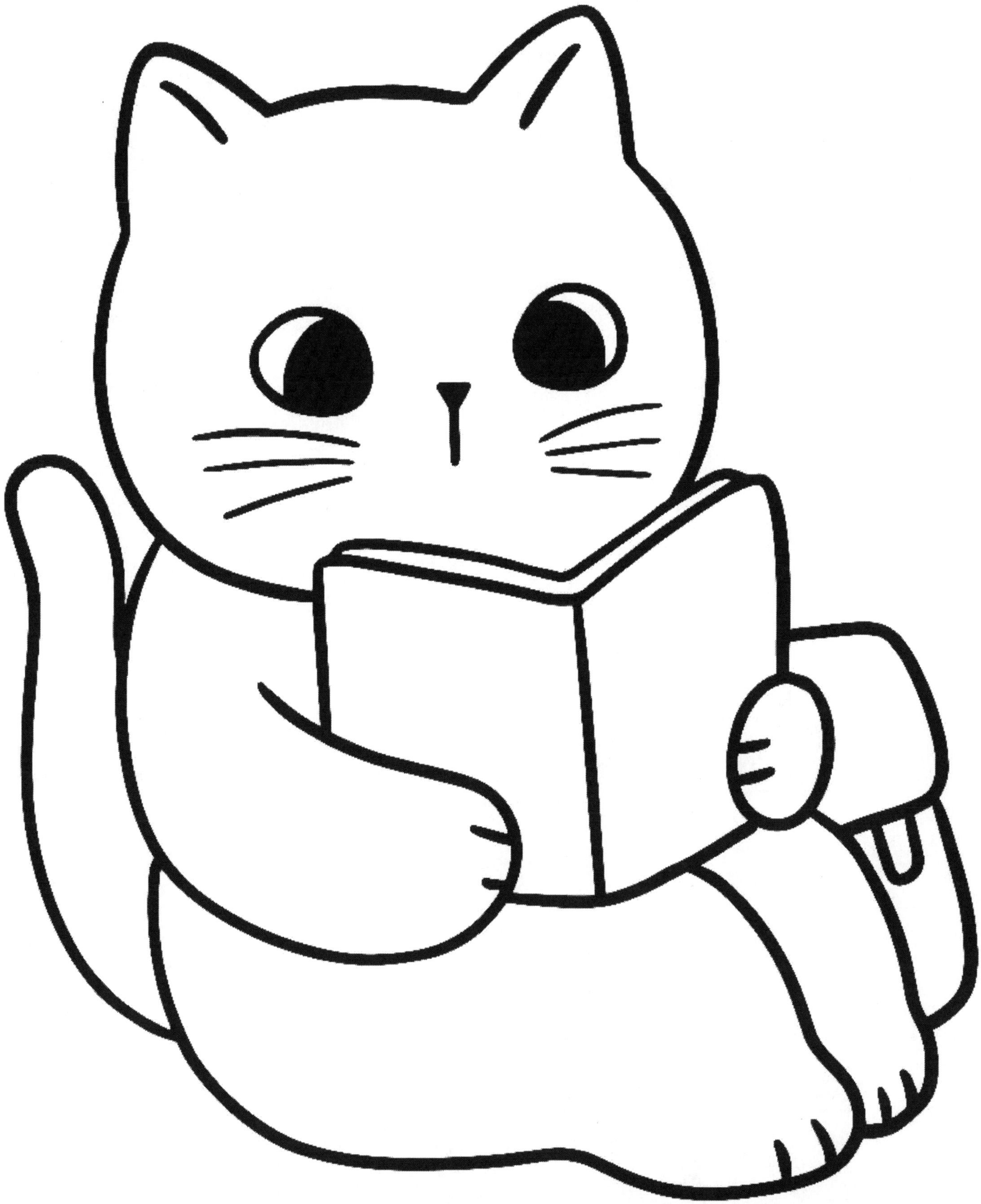

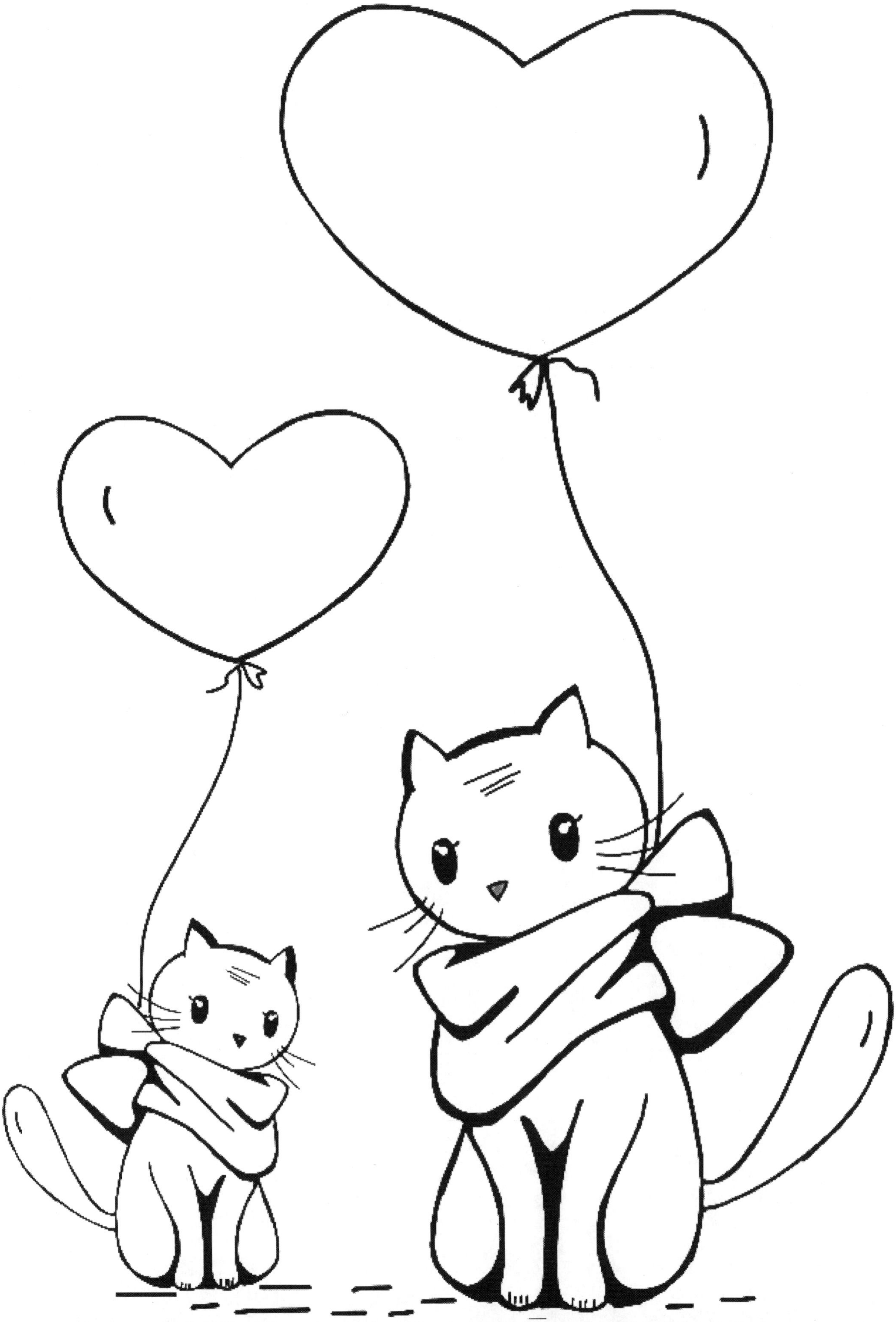

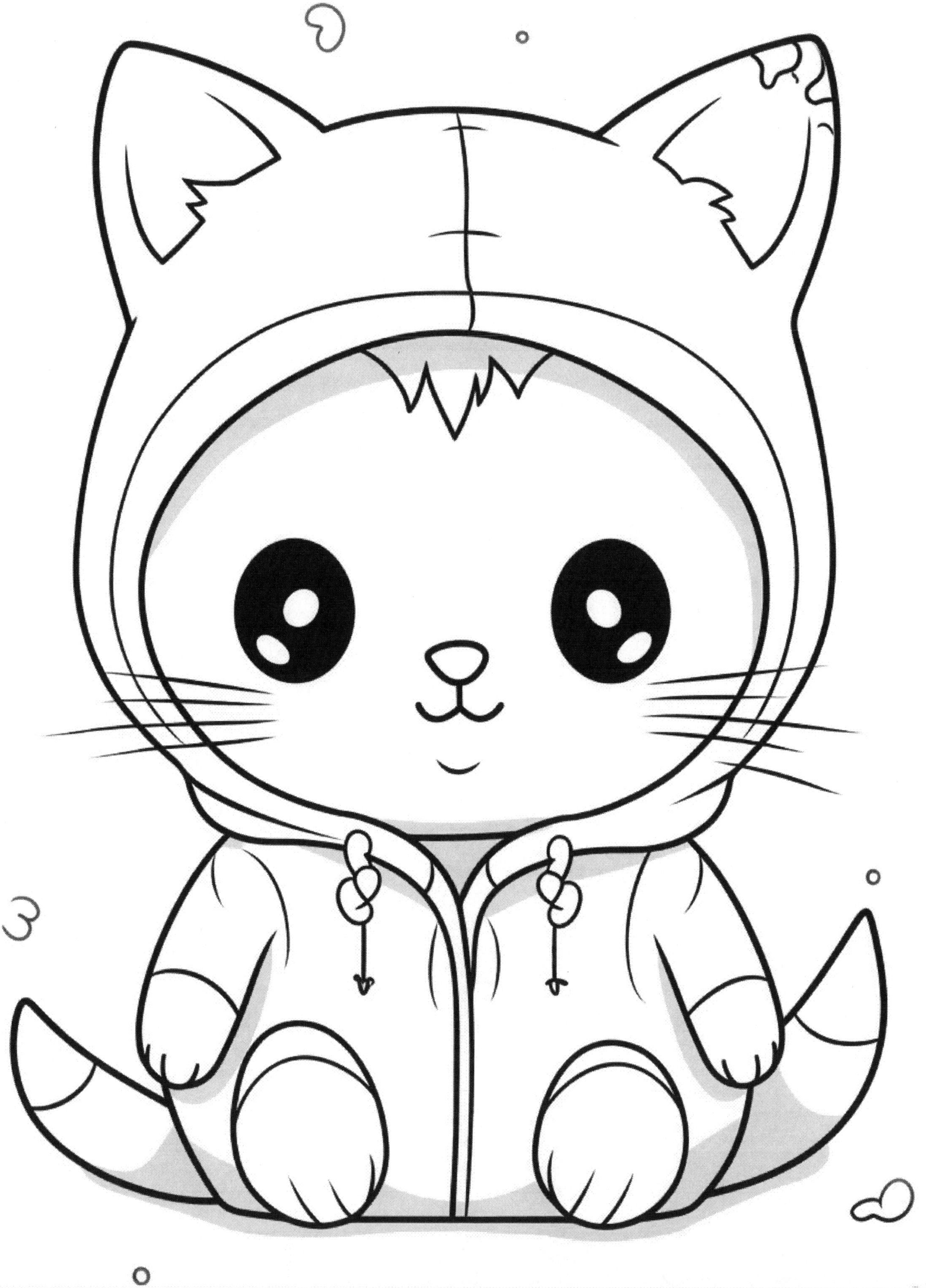

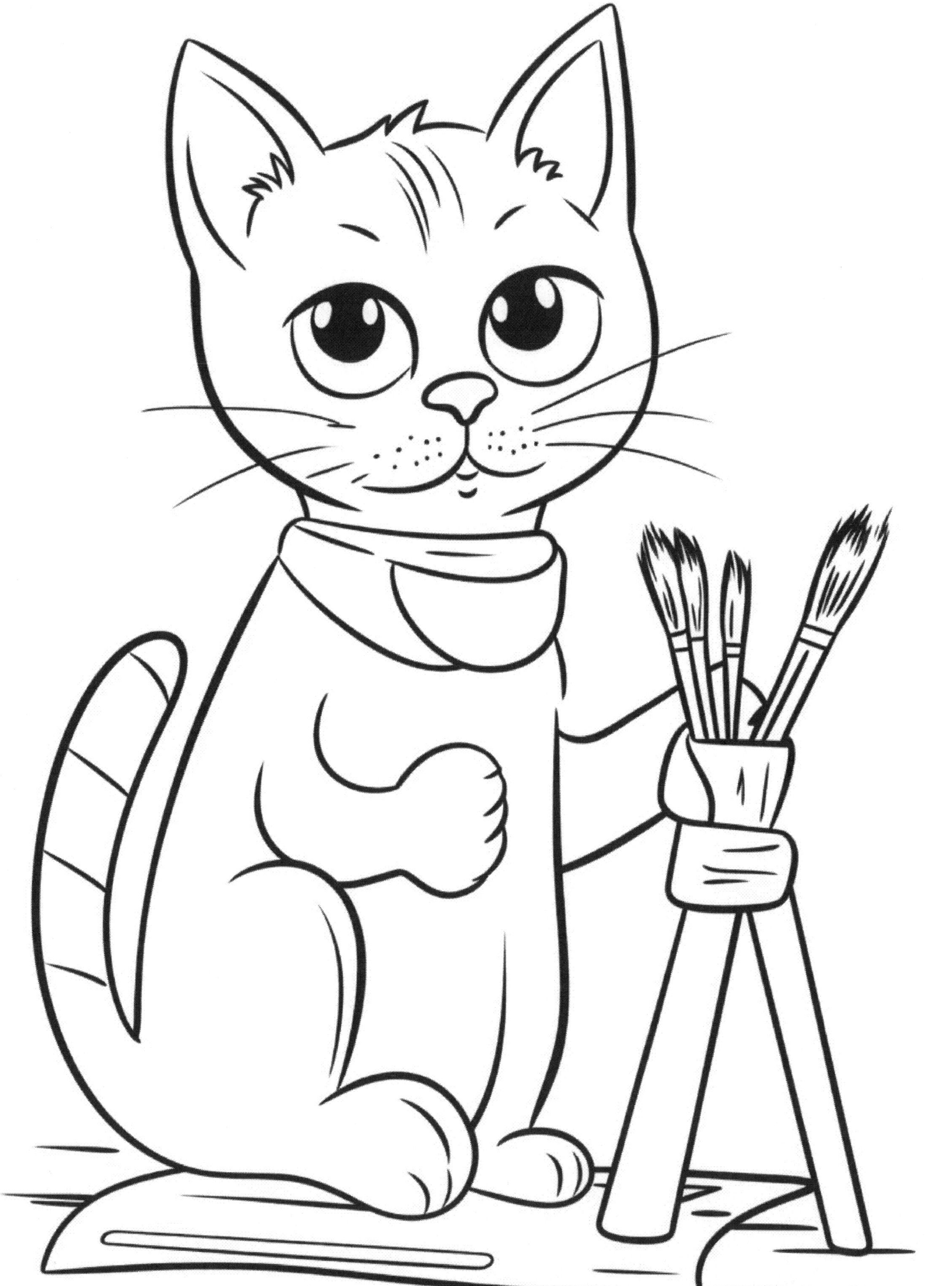

Made in the USA
Las Vegas, NV
16 December 2024

14428978R00031